Rock and Jazz

by Bud Hamilton
illustrated by Lynne Avril

Core Decodable 33

McGraw Hill Education

Bothell, WA • Chicago, IL • Columbus, OH • New York, NY

MHEonline.com

Send all inquiries to:
McGraw-Hill Education
8787 Orion Place
Columbus, OH 43240

ISBN: 978-0-02-145721-2
MHID: 0-02-145721-2

Printed in Canada.

9 10 11 12 KOD 24

In the attic, Jim has drums.

Jim hits his drums.

Jim's drumsticks hit and hit.

Bam! Bam! Bam!

Dad zips to the attic.

"I am in a rock band," said Jim.

In back, Madge has drums.

Madge hits the drums.

Bam! Bam! Bam!

Madge's drumsticks hit and hit.

Mom zips to the back.

"I am in a jazz band," said Madge.

Jim did not budge.
He just hits drums.

Madge did not budge.
Madge just hits drums.

Dad has a gift of muffs.

Mom has a gift of plugs.

Mom has on muffs.

Dad has his plugs.